AF583156

Dogs Day Out

A Countryside Adventure

ISBN: 978-1-3999-8993-0

Dedicated to the dogs who inspired this story -
The real Punda, Marmaduke and Diggle

It’s 8:30am on a sunny Wednesday in April. Grandpa is snoring softly in his armchair, a newspaper resting on his lap.

Granny Rose is getting ready to leave the house. She puts on her coat, grabbing an umbrella in case of any sudden rain showers.

‘Be good boys, I’ll be back soon’ she says to the dogs waiting patiently at her feet.

Reaching into her pocket she pulls out three biscuits in the shape of a bone.

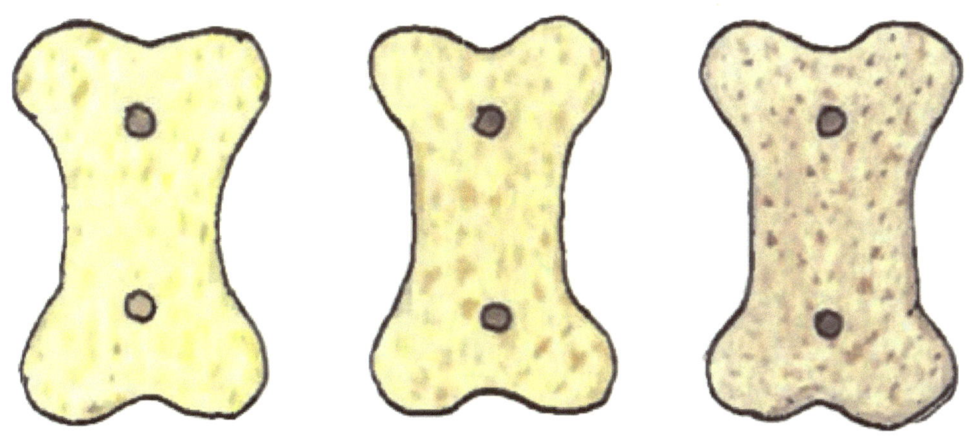

The dogs sit quickly, noses sniffing the air wildly.

The first biscuit goes to Punda. He sits up tall and lean, offering a delicate paw as he waits.

Next is Marmaduke. His ginger curls fall into his eyes as he looks up at her lovingly.

Last is Diggle, the smallest but by far the most eager. He wags his tail.

Granny turns and leaves, closing the door quietly behind her.

Marmaduke stretches out his front paws and yawns before plodding down the hallway, followed quickly by Punda.

‘No, no, no! You can’t go back to bed!’ squeals Punda as he trots closely behind.

Granny will be gone all morning and Grandpa is fast asleep, this may be our only chance this week to have an adventure!’

Having heard the word adventure Diggle comes speeding in, slipping on the wooden floor.

'I'd like to go exploring, there are so many new smells now that spring has sprung!'

He's shaking with excitement as he begs Marmaduke to come with them.

Marmaduke looks longingly at his warm bed when he suddenly gets a twinkle in his eye.

‘I’ll come… if we can go up White Horse Hill, it’s my favourite place in the world.’

Diggle gulps, his tail now between his legs.

He's been avoiding White Horse Hill so he doesn't have to face his fear of heights. It's a very big hill for someone as little as Diggle.

Marmaduke smiles and puts a caring arm around his little brother. There is no better way to rise above a fear than with your big brothers at your side.

'We'll do it together, as a team.'

Diggle thinks for a second and then nods slowly, a smile spreading across his face.

Marmaduke gives Punda a nudge as he sneaks quietly past Grandpa to the back door being careful not to wake him.

He uses his long nose to push down the handle and jimmy the door open (A skill he often uses to get into the biscuit cupboard!)

They scurry through the daffodils, under the garden gate and down the driveway, looking both ways before crossing the road into the village.

Heading towards the farm in need of directions they dash past the tractors to avoid being caught by farmer Roy.

Out of sight they sneak through the barn and into a nearby field, where some naughty lambs have crossed under the fence to escape from their mothers.

As the most athletic of the group, Punda comes to the rescue to help return the lambs.

He stretches his legs, takes a deep breath and springs into a run.

As fast as lightening he herds the giggling babies back under the fence and over to the food trough where their mothers wait.

Yippee thinks Punda as he comes to a slow, 'I just beat my personal best!'

The sheep are extremely happy to have their lambs back and offer to help the dogs find their way to White Horse Hill as a sign of thanks.

'Our flock is spread right across the countryside; we'll send out the signal to the rest of the sheep to guide you.'

Punda thanks the sheep and they continue on their quest following the soft sound of baaing.

They pass from one field to another, crossing bridges and wiggling through gates until they come to a woodland where the sound of the sheep can no longer be heard.

Diggle looks up at the sun shining through the trees, breathing in all the earthy smells.

Realising they are lost, the dogs venture further into the woods in search of help.

They are taken by surprise when suddenly, a pair of pheasants are flushed from the thicket followed closely by a fox.

The fox is on her way back from a night time trip to the nearby chicken farm.

She moves swiftly, keen to get back to the den where her cubs wait.

Most of the animals who live in this part of the woods are nocturnal and went to bed hours ago before the sun rose, so she is surprised to see three dogs stood in front of her.

Hesitant at first, Marmaduke approaches the fox.

He explains how they got lost on their adventure and why they need help to find their way so that Diggle can overcome his fear of heights by climbing White Horse Hill.

The fox looks at Diggle with softness in her eyes.

She explains that she too has a fear. Afraid of open spaces she rarely leaves the woodland in daylight to avoid bumping into any farmers.

She agrees to lead the dogs to the edge of the woodland where there is a rabbit warren close by.

Rabbits are extremely good navigators and can help guide them on the final part of their journey.

With a sigh of relief, they follow the fox through the undergrowth, over fallen logs, and through the bluebells where she points to a field nearby.

They thank the fox who wishes Diggle luck.

They soon find the entrance to the burrow and as the smallest of the trio, it is decided that Diggle will enter the warren to ask for directions.

In one swift move he shoots down the rabbit hole causing bunnies to leap from all different entrances.

A few minutes later Diggle emerges followed by a fury friend.

They are familiar with this particular rabbit who often pops into the garden to nibble on Granny's vegetables.

In exchange for regular access to the cabbage patch the rabbit agrees to help the dogs.

Their warren spans for miles underneath these fields and can lead them to their journeys end.

The ground begins to rumble as the rabbits' thump their way through the underground tunnels.

Marmaduke keeps an ear close to the ground, following the trail as they track the sound in and out of fields and under hedges.

After a short while the noise fades and they look up at the steps of Dragon Hill.

Marmaduke puts his nose in the air, turning his head from side to side giving a sniff. He can tell they're close from the smell of the wet chalk in the morning dew.

Punda and Marmaduke race up the steps followed by Diggle bounding as quicky as his little legs will take him.

Punda stops before a chalky spot on the ground, looking down at his paws now covered in white.

Legend has it that this is the spot where Saint George fought a dragon.

Where a drop of its blood hit the ground, nothing has ever grown.

Diggle begins to shake. Dragon, nobody said anything about a dragon! He jumps behind Punda for protection.

Standing tall behind them is the huge figure of a white horse etched deep into the side of the hill.

Diggle turns and gasps in wonder! Marmaduke looks up smiling. He trots off calling over his shoulder 'Come on boys, let's make it to the top!'

As Punda begins to follow, he notices Diggle is no longer with them.

'I'm afraid I won't be able to make it all the way up there...' He looks at the ground, head hanging low as Punda comes to stand beside him.

'Bravery and courage don't come from being wise like Marmaduke or from being big and fast like me. It comes from your heart, and yours is big enough for all of us.'

Diggle puffs out his chest, takes a deep breath and gathers his courage.

They'll do it together, one step at a time.

After a steep climb they reach the chalk horse. 'I did it!' says Diggle smiling. His brothers cheer for him, proud of his bravery.

They gaze at its beauty weaving through all the on-lookers, before finally stopping to rest on top of Uffington Castle.

This early Iron Age hillfort marks the highest point in the whole of Oxfordshire. They sit and stare, admiring the vale below.

‘You can see six counties from here you know.’

Diggle peeks up at Marmaduke, adoration filling his eyes. I’d like to be as smart as my big brother one day he thinks.

They stay a while longer, watching children fly kites and listening to the skylarks warbling above.

With one final look over the vast landscape they set off back home, running down the ridgeway, tails wagging in the midday sun.

That was one big adventure they think, hopefully there are many more to come!

The end.

www.ingramcontent.com/pod-product-compliance
Lightning Source LLC
LaVergne TN
LVHW071211160826
845679LV00003B/799

9781399989930